MANAGING YOUR WEALTH

A MUST-READ FOR AFFLUENT FAMILIES

CHRISTOPHER F. POCH

Christopher F. Poch
christopherpoch@gmail.com

More information at www.peaceofmindinvesting.net

ISBN: 978-1537118017

Photo Credits:
  Piotr Zajc / Shutterstock.com
  SZBDesign / Shutterstock.com
  Marco Rullkoetter / Shutterstock.com

To all of my family, friends, coaches, and mentors;
I am the sum total of your help and guidance.
Thank you.

Who we are today is not as important as who we may become tomorrow.

All net proceeds will be donated to the
Order of Malta Pilgrimage Foundation.

The purpose of the Foundation is to cover the expenses of maladies (sick, handicapped, wounded, and otherwise deprived individuals) and their caregivers so they can attend the annual Lourdes Pilgrimage in France.

www.pilgrimagefoundation.org

TABLE OF CONTENTS

WHY THIS BOOK IS FOR YOU

IN AN HOUR YOU CAN BECOME SMARTER ABOUT OVERSEEING YOUR WEALTH THAN 99% OF INVESTORS

———————◆•◆———————

You are likely reading this book because you have affluence and you want to be smart in how you manage it. Through devoting one hour's worth of time, you can read this book and become smarter about how to oversee your wealth than 99% of the investors out there. It took me over 30 years to learn what follows, and months to cut it down to advice that is understandable and actionable.

This book is a primer providing an outline to guide you through all of the matters to consider and provides the essential tools to develop your strategic plan. My intent is not to provide you answers to all the questions. The goal is simple: Give you enough to know what to look for and how to find the right team of advisors to help you do it. *The brevity of this book is its strength.*

This book is for the family with enough assets and responsibilities to merit paying attention to. Most of the advice applies to everyone, but all of it requires effort on behalf of the reader. I have worked with families with $100K to several billion and most issues are the same. For those who have over $5MM in investable assets, this is, in my humble opinion, a "must-read."

Who this book is *not* for

This book is not for the beginner who is starting to save. For you, the best advice I can offer comes from Ben Franklin's timeless quote: "A penny saved is a penny earned."

Each chapter is a standalone, with pertinent content. You will notice some overlap, but that is okay. This is intentional and reinforces how these topics are interrelated.

THE JOURNEY FROM STOCK BOY TO STOCK BROKER

THERE IS A STARTING POINT TO UNDERSTANDING WEALTH. IF YOU ARE FORTUNATE ENOUGH TO HAVE IT, YOU HAVE TO LEARN HOW TO MANAGE IT TO KEEP IT.

An overview of my journey that has brought me to this point seems to be in order. Those who understand my story gain a greater understanding about why I'm so committed to helping families manage their wealth effectively.

Today, I am well-known in the industry for advising ultra high net worth families (those with investable asset of $30MM and up). I didn't start here, however. My journey began much earlier in life. My first job came my way at the age of eight. I worked at my dad's store putting price labels on merchandise. Over time, I graduated to car loader, stock boy, cashier, paint salesman, and then I sold door-to-door. When it was time for college, I always had jobs during the school year and during summers I was a traveling salesperson, sold life insurance, and, at twenty-two, I started cold-calling at Merrill Lynch.

It's always been about solving problems

I remember hearing my dad tell us stock boys to never let a customer leave the store without bringing them to a salesperson (read — experienced adult), even if we didn't have the item in stock. He explained that, when a customer came in with ten things to buy, they really came in with ten problems to solve. As the saying goes, no one wants to own a drill — they want a hole.

Our job was to help the customer solve ten problems and avoid having to drive around town to get it done. I learned something about value and price. You didn't have to have the lowest price in order to provide the highest value. I didn't appreciate it at the time, but there is enormous value in being able to solve all of your problems with one engagement.

We all face the same problems managing our wealth. We don't want to buy stocks or mutual funds; we want to retire comfortably, pay for college, and if we have enough, we want to help others, educate the poor, endow a hospital, or cure cancer.

From financial advisor to client advocate

At Merrill Lynch, I started out as a bullpen broker and sold municipal bonds to unknown names in a telephone book. From there I evolved to investment consulting and, ultimately, to advising clients worth billions. Along the way I learned a lot.

As a financial services practitioner, I know there is a way to offer sound investment advice, provide excellent service at a reasonable price, and still make a profit for your company. That's what happens most of the time for most people. However, in order to ensure you have that experience, you need to know how to avoid being charged too much, while receiving too little and feeling gypped in the process.

Start with realistic objectives

In the highly competitive, zero-sum game of investments, it is very difficult to "outperform" the rest of the crowd over time. A realistic objective should be to make a fair return, net of costs, without taking too much risk in the process. That is my personal goal. Recall the old adage: Bulls make money, bears make money, and pigs get slaughtered.

Understand that managing wealth is more than just investments

Outside of investments lies the other half of managing wealth, that of managing a family's fortune. Basics include wills, trusts, insurance, retirement plans, education funds, taxes, cash flow, and budgeting. These are topics that may take a lifetime to master, but we need to know enough about them in order to do what should be done, while avoiding wasting time and money on things that are not necessary.

Always make sure you find the right fit

The vast majority of financial professionals work hard, are well-intentioned, and do the best job they know how to do. However, over the last 15 years, the financial industry's training has become heavily focused on compliance and understanding the changes in the law. Unfortunately, there has been a decrease in the money spent teaching advisors how to listen, learn, and advise. In order to ensure compliance and avoid billion-dollar fines, the industry has streamlined the client-engagement process to a standardized experience.

I think there is a better way. That is why I wrote this book. If you follow these steps, you have a better-than-average chance of a finding an exceptional team of advisors and having a superior client experience.

Why I wrote this book

It has been a long-time goal of mine to lay out a simple step-by-step guide that friends and family could follow to understand how to manage their financial affairs.

This book is for clients, not for people in the wealth management industry. Some industry participants will find fault with parts of it. In some cases, I point out situations and scenarios to avoid. In other cases, I stress that when your economic interest diverges from your advisor's economics, recommendations can and often do follow the economic interest of the advisor. However, there is good news.

Any experienced professional with advanced training can do well by their clients. This book should help you find those professionals.

I also believe that there is no better place for wealth accumulation than the United States. This is the greatest country in the world, and democracy and capitalism has gotten us here. The financial industry is a big part of capitalism and advising clients how to manage their wealth is a noble profession. However, like every profession, there are preferred ways to approach it, and some practitioners approach and implement it better than others.

It is my greatest hope that the contents in this book help you to find the best way for you and your family to manage your wealth.

My conclusions are my opinion and are based upon my experience, not indisputable facts.

PLANNING

"Sing like no one is listening;
love like you've never been hurt;
dance like nobody's watching."

— Satchel Paige

You Just Came into a Pile of Money, What's Next?

Where to start

———◆•◄———

In 32 years as an advisor, I regularly encounter people coming into the unfamiliar responsibility of overseeing significant wealth. This is usually from either selling a business or inheriting wealth. For illustration sake, let's go with the assumption it is more than $5MM, maybe a lot more. The question that looms large is: where do I start?

> *"It's always best to start at the beginning."*
>
> — Glinda the Good Witch, *Wizard of Oz*

In order to start, you need to know where you are, where you want to go, and then how to get there. Don't jump right into the investments. Start with a personal financial statement.

A Personal Financial Statement is a document, not a $10MM house or $300K car

The temptation is to splurge, and that is okay if it is within reason. Just be sure you don't take on too much too soon and end up with headaches and hassles from a collection of assets that may quickly feel like liabilities.

Down the road, you will need to think about how to protect these assets from spurious claims, former partners or spouses, managers, employees, etc. Depending upon the amount of publicity surrounding the liquidity event, you may be targeted for theft, cyber attacks, etc. For now, just getting the basic paperwork is enough.

Cash flow is king

Your CPA can prepare your personal financial statement (PFS) or you can do it yourself on a simple Excel spreadsheet. This is to determine how much cash you can expect to generate to support your lifestyle, and to keep your expenses in line. Your PFS should include your assets, liabilities, and net worth. It is helpful if the assets are broken down by legal owner. For the liquid assets, also note where they are held. The important thing is to know what you have, who controls it, and where it is custodied.

Do you need a financial plan?

Yes, we all do, but at this stage it doesn't have to be formal or in great detail. Too many people start the financial planning process only to abandon it because the time involved was more than they expected. To start, you only need to know the basics:

1. How much money you need to do what you want.

2. From where the cash flow will come.

Locate important documents

These include your wills, estate plans, powers of attorney, medical proxies, final directives, etc. Know the locations of insurance policies, company ownership agreements, partnership documents, and trust paperwork. You will want to revisit these with your advisors soon, but this is good for now.

Family first, finances follow

Any serious discussion about managing wealth has to start with its larger purpose and that invariably begins with your family. Throughout this book, every discussion will be from the perspective that accumulating financial assets is not the ultimate goal. Financial assets are tools to help accomplish personal goals.

- I encourage you to spend 30 minutes with your spouse or partner and write down your thoughts to get alignment with each other. This step is powerful and very important, yet it is surprising how infrequently it is done.

Each person should list:

- Values, philosophies, or beliefs. What do you want your grandchildren to know about you?

- Life and family goals

- Financial goals

- Community or philanthropic goals

Compare notes and work toward a common list for your family. This conversation should help assure you are starting on the same page, heading in the same direction, and are happy about where you end up. When you are in agreement, the rest of the process goes more smoothly.

With your goals aligned, you can better know what you need to do to reach them. Congratulations, this puts you far ahead of most people. The question to ask now is: Should I seek a wealth advisor to help me do all of this or do I want to do it alone?

Using a wealth advisor or going it alone

Questions to ask a wealth advisor:

- How can you alleviate 70% of the hassles associated with managing wealth?

- Do you have a network of industry-leading professionals so I won't have to vet dozens of people personally?

- Can you help me think about asset allocation outside of stocks, bonds, and liquid investments? Real estate? Investments in private companies?

- What experience do you have with specialty items, such as art advisory and curatorial management, kidnap and ransom insurance, collections, offshore trust and tax, private placement insurance, dynasty trusts?

- Will I earn above-average investment returns? (This is a bit of a trick question. Be leery of advisors who exude too much confidence about beating the stock market. It is hard to do.)

Hire an experienced wealth advisor

To me, it is a no brainer. Engaging a qualified advisor to assist you in overseeing and managing your family's wealth will save you thousands of hours and almost certainly lots of money. The next chapter will offer thoughts on the processes associated with selecting an advisory team.

Unsolicited advice: Happiness and striving for success

Priorities and to-do lists, goals and action plans, schedules, and milestones fill our days and our lives. Our lists can seem endless and the demands on our time can be overwhelming. Is that what we were seeking when we started pursuing our life and career ambitions? It seldom is. So what do we do? Let's start by defining success.

Most people think about success as being connected with their family and community, feeling secure about the future, and having the time and resources to help others. So how do we achieve this amid the hectic day-to-day? A few thoughts to consider:

a. **Start each day being grateful** for the people we have in our lives. This brings peace and balance to our thinking. It also conditions our mind to see the good and even the benefits of setbacks.

b. **Focus on the important things** that will bring great joy when they are realized. Odds are high you will focus on your family first and somewhere later on down the list will come your finances.

c. **Write letters** to your spouse, family, friends, and children to let them know how much you love and appreciate them. It is a gift that will far out last a lifetime.

Letter to Clients Searching for a Wealth Advisor

Know what to look for and get what you need

———•◦•———

If you have decided to seek a new wealth advisor, permit me to offer a simple way to go about it. This process is the same for most asset levels; however, I have included several questions and topics that apply primarily to families with more than $10MM.

Know what you need. Consider these 30 points:

1. **Don't just ask friends.** Their opinions reflect their preferences and experience. If you do ask friends, at a minimum, also find out why they made their selection and how it compared with other options. If their process was not highly researched, disregard.

2. **Write it down.** Start by writing down your thoughts about the services and investment products you need, and what you want your relationship to be like. Adopt the mindset that you want to get the most value out of your advisor, not to pay the least.

3. **Select your advisors, then your investments.** Invest the time and attention to this part of the process, and do it well. Your team of tax, trust, and legal professionals will have a significant impact on the ultimate size of your estate. However, since most people focus on investments, I'm primarily addressing the investment part of wealth management.

4. **Determine your wealth-advisory needs.** Do you require financial planning, estate planning, and trust services? Will you need insurance, philanthropic, and tax planning advisory? Ascertain if the firms you are considering have extensive departments or just a few people assigned to cover a number of areas and a lot of clients? Are the services comprehensive, or are they glorified questionnaires to get to a sale? How involved do you want or expect the specialists to be? Do you want a licensed professional or an experienced counselor with an advanced degree?

5. **Products.** Do you want to make investments, buy insurance, get home loans, and credit cards all at the same place? Or, do you prefer providers with specialties and focused expertise? Do you want investment options offered by money managers unaffiliated with your advisor, or the customization of "in-house" investment strategies overseen by your own portfolio manager? Internally managed investment strategies are more profitable to the provider and advisors rarely fire themselves. However, "best-in-class" external investments don't always live up to their billing either.

6. **Client experience.** You have had great client experiences and poor ones. Write down the names of companies you love best and why. What do they do to consistently earn your trust? Write down your expectations for the types and frequency of contact you expect from your wealth advisor. Ask how quickly they return calls and emails, especially over the weekend.

Assessing your client experience

If the client experience is driven by an individual's promises, things can change. If it is driven by systems and a firm-wide attention to detail, you are in the right spot. Look for firms with systems that assure satisfaction. You can determine this through their business models.

The business model of the firm you select will influence your experience. All business models have benefits and limitations. The key to deliver a great experience will rest largely in the hands of the specific team you select. Common business models:

    a. **Large banks:** Firms with a broad array of products may be preferred for those who prize choice and convenience. Staff tends to be less experienced and the loading of clients per person tends to be higher.

    b. **Brokerage firms:** The client experience is almost entirely dependent upon the team of professionals serving the relationship. The model skews heavily toward investments. Planning services for estate, tax, and trust are usually secondary, often disconnected from your normal point of contact.

    c. **Trust companies:** These legal entities are almost always attached to a bank or asset management firm. The better ones have extensive internal trust, tax, and planning expertise. Investment results can vary widely.

    d. **Asset managers:** These firms mostly sell their own money-management services. Some offer outside money management, as well. Assess whether the included wealth-management services offer adequate breadth and expertise.

    e. **Insurance companies:** Advisors who are compensated primarily by insurance product sales use the term wealth management as a marketing tool. If you need to save and protect, insurance advisors may be perfect.

    f.   **Registered investment advisors:** Independent companies most often affiliate with one or more large custodians for products and support. They are independent by design and operate under a fiduciary standard. The segregated operational aspect adds a level of administrative complexity.

**Caveats

- **UHNW units.** Some large firms have special units to serve ultra high net worth families. The units tend to be staffed by more sophisticated, better-trained professionals. If your circumstances fit, seek out these units.

- **Regulatory filings.** Check out all firms, especially small ones.

7. **Local advisory team.** In large measure, your experience rests in the hands of the team you select or which is assigned to you. The lead person sets the tone, so don't worry too much about the other members. Assess whether the team members have sufficient technical expertise and formalized systems in place to ensure a superior experience. Ask:

    a.   Which services are provided, how frequently and by whom, and who initiates?

    b.   Who receives the call on weekends and when can I expect that call to be returned?

    c.   Request tangible samples of work product that meets the complexity of your needs.

8. **Intangible services.** Get a sense of the firm and team's commitment to the intangible services. Who will educate me, help me grow and learn, and be smarter about money, investing, taxes, budgeting, philanthropy, and family governance? Real pros will have answers to these questions and examples ready.

9. **Compensation drives behavior.** Know how the advisory team gets paid. Are the fees you pay the same regardless of asset allocation and product recommendation? If not, do in-

ternal product fees offset the overarching advisory fee? Does the compensation of the team vary based upon asset allocation or product recommendations? Alternative investments, structured notes, and insurance are usually not included in these fees. If multiple fees can be layered, be leery. Know what the fees are and how the layering of fees can occur. When your economic interest diverges from your advisor, the recommendations usually follow the economic interest of the advisor.

10. **Low fees are great, but avoid the bait-and-switch.** When it is all said and done, high-quality wealth management firms will charge between .75% and 1.5% on assets under management in most relationships. If the fee is lower, ask where and how the firm is making up the difference — because they are. Understand when, why, and how recommendations can move from a lower fee to higher fee. High fees reduce your net worth, so avoid them. *However, a rock-bottom fee sentences you to inexperienced staff and call-center-quality service.* Ask yourself, "Is this what I really want?"

11. **Minimum relationship size.** Relationship minimums indicate familiarity with relevant issues, professional training, and service focus. The higher the minimum, the fewer the number of clients per advisor, and the more specialized the attention you are likely to receive. If the firm has the right resources and the local team meets your standards, you have a good chance of having a favorable experience.

12. **Interview candidates.** Contact the manager of the office and describe what you are seeking. Be clear that you don't want the person who is next up on the "lead call-in list," nor the highest-revenue producer. Firms try to rotate new client opportunities to keep employees happy, not necessarily to match your needs. Meet with the manager and the lead advisor of the team. A room filled with six team members shows depth and breadth, but it also could imply a bunch of product specialists who are motivated to get the most out of you.

13. **Take notes and record what you heard.** Write it down. It's challenging to recall all the nuances and details that you learn during these meetings.

The one essential step no one does

14. **After your meetings.** Compose a summary of your notes and email it to the advisor and the manager. Ask for clarification on points where you are unsure if you understood what they meant. This one step, which is skipped by all, can be the difference between understanding what you will receive and your chances of having a good experience, versus that of disappointment.

If the response from the advisor is clear and direct — good. If the response is ambiguous, buried in attachments, or references legalistic language, beware. Regulations limit what can be written, but most service questions can be answered directly.

List what you know about investing and what you don't

15. **Investor behavior drives results.** How you behave during turbulent markets will determine your wealth accumulation. Most buy high and sell low. In order to earn competitive results, you must educate yourself, be patient, and resist panic when markets perform poorly.

16. **Ask how your advisors will educate you and keep you calm when others are not.** Risk and fees are important, but don't let the tail wag the dog. Pay your people well so you will get their best.

Understanding the nuances

Now that you have the checklist and the process, let's go a little deeper to explore nuances.

17. **Investment, income tax, trust and estate law, insurance.** Your team of advisors should cover the array of important matters and should have enough knowledge to discuss the recommendations of their colleagues. Income tax, estate tax, insurance, and investments are the core four areas. With larger, more complex families, a retained general counsel can be a big plus.

18. **Planning is everyone's job.** Having a comprehensive and co-ordinated plan is critical. The challenge is to combine the interwoven objectives with the myriad of strategies and tactics. There are usually a half dozen ways to accomplish one's goals and no one way is perfect. The real trick is to avoid strategies that are expensive to maintain or difficult to unwind.

It is not uncommon for some planners with good intentions to recommend aggressive strategies with high return potential. In these cases, it is essential that you have a complete discussion on risk. Overlapping expertise among your advisory team increases the probability of getting the right plan in place the first time.

Services

19. **Finding the right balance.** Not every client wants the "platinum" package with the attendant expenses, but no one wants an impersonal relationship with someone who dispenses advice in a vacuum. The integration of your advisors and how frequently you interact with them will vary. Assess how proactive your wealth management team will be and how well they will interact with your other advisors outside of their firm.

Compensation for sales or satisfaction

20. Sales. Employees' compensation structure gives insight into how the relationship is likely to unfold. Companies that pay employees based upon product sales or net asset increases often tend to have employees that contact clients to "make them aware of investment opportunities"— a/k/a, sell them something. Clients are often surprised to learn how common this is.

21. Satisfaction. Firms that pay employees based upon client satisfaction, and do not have quotas based upon new clients or new assets tend to attract a different kind of employee. Look for a mechanism to regularly gauge your satisfaction with their service.

Investment results

22. Always difficult to compare. Most firms only highlight their best-performing investment strategies or funds. Strategies with poor performance are quietly shut down or eliminated. Hence, you can never compare apples to apples, and even if you could, past performance shows how that investment did in an environment that is unlikely to be similar to the one just ahead.

23. Seeking alignment. It is helpful to know whether most people with similar objectives are invested in a uniform strategy or model. In cases where everyone gets the same "cooking," customization is nearly impossible. If the results were suboptimal, it simply indicates everyone suffered together.

24. Evaluating investment proposals. At some point you will receive a proposal complete with investment recommendations and impressive past performance. Know that the specific investments were recommended because they met your objectives and had one of the highest risk-adjusted recent performances.

25. *Footnote on footnotes. Take a close look at the footnotes, especially when comparisons are made to custom benchmarks with long disclosures. Custom benchmarks with long disclosures, and whose composition changes, might indicate mathematical gymnastics were necessary to achieve favorable comparisons.

Fees

26. **All-in costs.** It is important to know what the "all-in" costs will be and how the costs may change as the portfolio changes. Some firms entice prospects by initially recommending low-cost index funds or ETFs, or say they won't charge fees on bond portfolios or structured notes. This may be true, but beware. Bonds and structured notes are traded with the commission included in the net price. The only way to be sure that a "bait-and-switch" doesn't happen to you is to select a firm where it can't happen.

27. **Broker, advisor, or fiduciary?** Advisors operating on a commission basis, in my opinion, open themselves up to criticism. Registered investment advisors (RIAs) and advisors working under an RIA have a higher standard of duty. Ask yourself: "Do I want to spend time checking the markets and keeping up with economic trends, or do I want to be served by a fiduciary required to have my best interests come first and foremost?" If there is no economic incentive to influence recommendations, you should be okay.

Number of providers to consider

28. **Avoid horse races.** Every company would like all of your business, but almost all will accept a partial assignment. Having more than one provider can be a good idea, but only if you are willing to invest the time to balance what you hear from the various providers and sift through the differences. Be careful not to set up a performance "horse race" between providers. In order to win the rest of your business, or to avoid losing what

they have, advisors can be motivated to covertly engage in a performance race. Risk can seep into your portfolios.

29. **In my opinion…select one.** Despite the limitations, I usually recommend selecting one high-quality wealth management firm. Give them the mandate to manage the entire relationship and enlist the tax, insurance, and other advisors to be the "watchdogs." The other advisors will know if the wealth advisor is doing a good job or not. Once a year, ask all advisors for their opinion of each other. Be direct. Good advisors will tell you the truth. Weak advisors should be replaced.

30. **Get accountability and avoid brown paint.** To some, this may sound like putting all your eggs in one basket but I don't see it that way. To me, it is the best way to get accountability and judge whether you are getting what you want and deserve. My Dad, a lifelong hardware man, was fond of saying, "If too many people are mixing the paint, all you end up with is brown paint."

How to Assemble an A-Team of Advisors

A STEP-BY-STEP GUIDE TO BUILD YOUR STRATEGIC ADVISORY TEAM

———————●———————

Selecting the right team to advise you on strategic issues is as important to your wealth as your investment selections.

Why this is it so important

Building a home requires an architect, engineers, plumbers, electricians, roofers, and another dozen specialists to deliver a safe and sound household in which to live. The same principle applies in assembling a team of capable advisors to secure your family's financial foundation. For this discussion, I will focus on the needs of families with moderate to high complexity.

CPAs

1. **Know what you need.** Do you want financial reports and budgets prepared for several entities? Do you have LLCs, trusts, partnerships, scheduled gifting, a family foundation, and business interests in different states? As you add complexity, an understanding of the interrelationships and tax treatments becomes increasingly important.

2. **Aren't all CPAs the same?** Tax laws are the same and the software that most CPAs use is similar. Important differentiators are training, professional experience, and familiarity with unique items. Membership in the American Institute of CPAs (AICPA) is a good start. The ACIPA also awards a Personal Financial Specialist designation, which indicates an additional level of knowledge and training.

3. **Local firm, boutique, or "Big Four?"** Firms with national and international presences with public company clients are often conflicted out of representing senior officers. If your needs are complex, and especially if you are exposed to international tax law, they may be a good option. Most clients will do well with local or regional tax firms. If you are subject to taxes in multiple states, ask about their state and local tax (SALT) capabilities.

Trust and estate attorneys

Among the many considerations are state licensing, advanced certifications, and general experience. Participation in the American Bar Association Section of Real Property, Trust, and Estate Law or the state bar is a good sign. A coveted peer-awarded designation is Fellow of the American College of Trust and Estate Counsel (ACTEC). There are many, many excellent attorneys who are not affiliated with these organizations. Some are extremely sophisticated legal generalists and others are managing partners of white-shoe firms. However you choose to evaluate your attorney's selection, have a thoughtful process.

Insurance professionals

Insurance gets a bad rap. It is something we all need that no one wants to pay for. The bad rap is probably largely due to the wide range of talent and expertise that exists among life insurance agents and brokers. Fortunately, there are many qualified professionals who can add value to your estate and financial planning team.

Accreditations. Most tenured professionals will be Chartered Life Underwriters or Accredited Estate Planners and members of several national associations. Most industry designations demonstrate knowledge and expertise; however, membership in some organizations reflects sales success. It's helpful to know the difference.

Company-affiliated or independent? Insurance agents are employees of insurance companies and their loyalty is to that insurance company. Brokers are typically independent and can offer products from several companies, but many agents also can serve as brokers. You have to learn what to look for.

For starters, ask for an in-depth analysis of your current policies, and it should be objective, not just focusing on reasons to replace your coverage. The analysis should show how a strategy works in conjunction with different estate planning strategies. If they can't analyze your policies and don't have the ability to illustrate how different strategies work, they probably don't work with complex families on a regular basis.

Finally, seek out professionals who are happy to share their recommendations with your advisors. People who are reluctant may be recommending something that, although suitable, may not be optimal.

Overlapping expertise

Assemble a team that is familiar with practices of other team members. Overlapping expertise protects you from recommendations that, for whatever reason, don't make sense.

> **Example:** There can be tension between advisors about which strategy or products should be used to accomplish the same goal. This is especially true with insurance, but also applies to private investments, hedge funds, and local real estate.

The tax advantages of insurance contracts make it the playground for creative strategies and complicated structures. Of concern is the long-term nature of implementing an insurance strategy. One needs to be sure any strategy selected will still be right for you long after the commission has been paid. Good insurance professionals understand how to match products with liquidity needs and changing tax laws.

You never call me— the #1 Achilles Heel of service

CPAs and attorneys are at the top of the trust chain for good reason. They don't actively market their services, only bill for their time and are bound by high industry ethical standards.

However, this strength can be their weakness.

Since most people don't want to receive a call and then get a bill in the mail, lawyers and CPAs have grown reluctant to initiate client contact. As a result, they are frequently brought into the discussion only after important decisions have been made.

The client may lament their choice and the advisor wonders why clients don't call prior to important decisions. The advisor takes the blame, but the client has to live with the outcome.

Solution: A Senior Strategic Advisor (SSA)

Primary point of contact. Look for one professional to take on the responsibility as your primary advisor to navigate and integrate the myriad of issues and options. He or she should be a seasoned, experienced professional who will proactively contact you whenever there is information, actions, or recommendations to be considered.

Facilitator, not bottleneck. The Senior Strategic Advisor (SSA) is the "go-to" advisor for all things family and financial. He or she is responsible for the communication among all of the family's legal, tax, and insurance advisors. To the extent possible, he/she ensures that all subject matter experts proactively communicate with you in a timely fashion.

Breadth and depth of knowledge. The SSA must be knowledgeable across disciplines to be effective in understanding and communicating concepts at a high level, and must remain "current" through ongoing continuing education. The SSA participates in important meetings with other advisory team members.

Enhanced communication. The SSA establishes the regular communications the client should expect: Face-to-face meetings, conference calls, topical updates, event invitations, newsletters, etc. When you find your Senior Strategic Advisor, the rest will be easy.

HOW TO DE-RISK BUYING INSURANCE

KNOWLEDGE WITH TRANSPARENCY IS THE BEST POLICY

There can be a big difference between people who sell insurance and insurance professionals. Whomever you use, be sure they are *professionals*.

The basics

The question of insurance — what type and how much — has long been debated. Gone are the days of the agent going door-to-door on Fridays to collect the weekly premium to cover burial costs. Today, insurance plays a much larger and more sophisticated role in protecting one's assets.

Whether life, long-term care, or property and casualty insurance, the central questions to answer are: What risks am I exposed to? How much exposure do I have? And, should I pay someone else to assume that risk?

Life insurance

Plan first, then insure. If the life insurance is for liquidity to pay estate taxes, have your estate attorney help you decide how to minimize your taxable estate and then insure the anticipated liability. If there are income needs or other purposes, the amount will be larger.

How much? In my opinion, work with a professional who does not get paid on life insurance commissions such as a CPA or investment person, in conjunction with your insurance professional, to help determine how much you need. If the purpose of insurance is income replacement, it could be 10-15 times your income, depending on your other assets and future expenses such as college, weddings, etc.

Universal life, term, and flexible premium are three common types of insurance contracts that meet certain needs. Some contracts rely on investment returns to keep premiums down. In these cases, understand what might happen if the stock market goes down a lot, as it did in 2008. Insurance policies that relied on stock market returns required substantial contributions to avoid failing. It is often at these times of duress when liquidity is scarce and people don't have the cash.

How life insurance should be owned

It's complicated. It varies by purpose so let's start with the basics. Among the most common ways life insurance policies are owned is through an Irrevocable Life Insurance Trust (ILIT). This is a legal entity where the beneficiary is also the trust and therefore the proceeds are not subject to estate taxes. This structure also facilitates multi-generational planning while providing valuable asset protection from creditors and/or spousal issues. There are too many nuances to fully explore here, but implementation is relatively easy, and the costs to set up and maintain an ILIT, if done properly, are minimal.

From whom to buy

Straightforward planning and a modest amount. If your needs are fairly standard, most insurance agents will do a fine job. However, they may be limited to the policies that are offered by the companies with whom they are appointed. In most cases, the MetLife agents can only offer MetLife polices and the Northwestern Mutual agent the same thing. All good agents will offer you their best product to address your needs. If possible, have another informed professional help you assess which policies meet your needs best.

Complex estate planning. If you have a complicated estate plan with multiple entities that rely on payments, loans, or waivers to fulfill the estate planning strategy, having a competent professional in charge is a must. That can be an insurance professional, lawyer, CPA, or wealth advisor. Since it will require coordination among several of the advisors, however, one person needs to be responsible.

Jumbo policies. For those few who need to insure large amounts (over $100MM), the industry will often pool the risk among several companies. Using an agent who does this type of underwriting on a regular basis is a must.

No Jack-of-all-trades. Be especially careful of the person who can sell life insurance, advise on investments, and file your taxes "all under one roof." The adage, ".... master of none," probably applies.

Property and casualty insurance

It is common for people to have multiple homes, boats, jewelry, art, and special items. Many own these assets in different names, in different states, and are insured by different companies. Some have coastal vacation properties and others have commercial rentals. Figuring out the maze of how to properly insure it is difficult and takes time. Commercial insurance is very different, and therefore, I will only address the personal lines.

Understanding gaps, avoiding overlaps. It seems like every month new risks are identified. The result is that either insurance premiums go up or exclusions are built into the language of future policies. Risks with special nuances include mold, wind, environmental, cyber, identification theft, and kidnapping. People who are insured by different carriers run the risk of having incomplete or uncoordinated coverage.

National brokers. If you have a complex asset base and the attendant risks, seek out a national brokerage firm that is licensed to sell coverage of all your risks in all the states you need. In a perfect world, you can get a fairly priced comprehensive policy from one carrier. This reduces the risk of two companies pointing the finger at the other in regards to which company will pay, should a loss occur. Alternatively, your broker will know how to optimally align the coverage.

Periodic reviews. Every few years it is worth reviewing what is and is not covered under your policies. Like a dental appointment for a regular cleaning, it is good for you. A friend of mine had regular homeowner's insurance with a reputable company for fifteen years. Out of the blue, they had water run onto their property because of construction on a neighboring property. The damage to their basement was not covered. No one could have expected that.

Coverage amount and deductibles

Most property risks, like home and auto, are insurable only up to the amount of loss or replacement. With liability coverage, umbrella and other insurance, you usually can determine how much you need, and therefore how much coverage you should get.

Large deductibles lower premiums. In most cases, you can choose how large a deductible you want before your insurance kicks in. If you have a low deductible and submit a lot of smaller claims your insurance company may increase your premiums. Determine how large a loss you can withstand and weigh if a reduction in premiums is worth taking the risk of increasing your deductible.

Know your break even. There is a break-even point where the savings in the annual premium equals the increase in the deductible. Often it is around three to four years. Those who are inclined to self-insure may want to have higher deductibles and lower premiums.

Long Term Care (LTC)

The first item to evaluate is what type of LTC do you want and do the facilities meet your needs. Then compare policies to see whether the coverage that meets your needs is affordable. Policies can be quite complicated with many options and restrictions. Many affluent families prefer to pay for home health care despite the very high costs. With health care costs soaring, every family is well advised to investigate if it makes sense to buy coverage and to compare at least three carriers.

Final thoughts

This chapter has focused on an area of financial wellbeing that few pay much attention to, and only learn of deficiencies after something bad happens. A word to the wise, find a knowledgeable insurance professional who can help you through the nuances and review your coverage every three to four years.

INVESTING

You never actually own a Patek, Philippe. You merely take care of it for the next generation.

So it is with generational wealth.

How to Manage Your Family's Fortune

Whether you have $1MM or $100MM

———•—

Working with over 550 ultra high net worth families and advising tens of billions in assets, I have seen what works. Generational wealth must be properly structured with trusts, but once the money is where it should be, this is how you should approach investing it.

The proper mindset

1. **Adopt a capital preservation focus.** Preserving capital is the first step toward growing it. A focus on absolute return, not relative return, is key to achieving this goal.

2. **Avoid permanent losses.** Define risk as the likelihood of permanent impairment of capital, as opposed to price volatility, and make every effort to avoid large losses so that your wealth can compound at attractive rates over time. The power of compounding wealth is enormous.

3. **Value orientation.** Investing with a margin of safety, that is to say investing at a discount to intrinsic value, is key. When valuations are high, don't underestimate the value of holding

cash, despite the short-term drag on performance. Cash gives one peace of mind and a host of choices.

4. **Fundamentals count.** Finding great businesses at the right price is rare, and when you find one you want to make sure you own them in size. In my opinion it is better to own shares of 25 great companies than to own shares in 100 companies, 75 of which you don't like quite as much as the top 25.

5. **Diversification.** Once you are wealthy, the goal typically is to stay wealthy. Owning an array of assets minimizes the risk of unexpected events that could be damaging to your life style and future prospects. The core four areas of concern are:

   • Stocks

   • Bonds

   • Cash

   • Real estate

Within each category, especially stocks, diversity and depth are important.

6. **Ownership orientation.** Long-term investors who can withstand interim volatility should maintain an ownership posture. That is to say, buy stocks. Over time, stocks are a better hedge against inflation than bonds and provide a greater opportunity to achieve attractive absolute returns.

7. **Long-term view.** Short-term performance is unpredictable. The surest path to generating attractive investment returns is to maintain a long-term focus. This allows one to patiently wait for the realization of value without being swayed by market volatility. It also reduces unnecessary portfolio turnover, which detracts from returns.

8. **Partnerships and aligned interests.** Seek out situations where the principals are invested alongside you and pay the same fees. If it is good for the goose, it should be good for the gander.

Assets you want to own

Look for companies with all, or most, of the following business and financial attributes:

1. **Essential products and services.** It is exciting to buy stock in the next blockbuster drug or disruptive technology company, but they usually don't work out as well as hoped or planned. It is safer to own companies that sell products and services that people need in both good and bad economic times.

2. **Loyal customers.** Great companies have loyal customers who are not lured away by a temporarily discounted price. Loyal customers know they will get value.

3. **Leadership in an attractive market niche or industry.** Most people do what other people do assuming the wisdom of crowds. When an industry expands, the leaders enjoy a disproportionate share of the growth, and when it shrinks the smaller players go out of business.

4. **Sustainable competitive advantages.** Lower costs, better technology, patent protection, as well as reputation for service and quality are all reasons why great franchises have staying power.

5. **High returns on invested capital.** Industries that do not require continual capital investments in order to grow are where the greatest earnings compounding opportunities exist.

6. **Strong free cash flow.** Companies that can generate high free cash flow have flexibility to make investments to improve service, quality, lower costs, and have access to capital to make attractive acquisitions.

7. **Great people.** Seek to invest in companies whose managers have high levels of integrity, are excellent operators, and are good capital allocators.

8. **When to buy.** When a company meets these criteria, buy the stock when its market price reaches 75% or less of the intrinsic value. In general, if a company passes these tests and is cheap, own it.

9. **When to sell.** This is probably the most difficult question. Since no one can predict which company will become the next Google or Amazon, prudence dictates systematically reducing risk. When a position significantly exceeds its intrinsic value, or becomes twice the size of the average holding, sell some.

Should I just buy an index fund?

Proponents of index funds and ETFs are quick to point out that passively managed portfolios have historically outperformed two-thirds of actively managed US equity portfolios. Given this record, how can you be confident that the approach described above can outperform passive products over a full market cycle?

The answer is threefold: Diversification, valuation, and investment criteria. To understand, look at the results experienced by index investors and those who do not adhere to a disciplined process, not the index result itself.

Index investing's dirty little secret

Most investors claim to be long-term oriented, but their actual behavior suggests otherwise. Investors tend to pour more money into index funds and ETFs (as well as other equity products) after several years of strong equity performance. Investors then typically lose confidence when markets decline and withdraw capital near market bottoms. Legendary investor Stan Druckenmiller observed a "buy and hold strategy beats trying to time the market because 85% of people do worse than random."[1] The problem is people just don't stick to it.

As a result, the return for the average investor in an index fund has historically been much worse than the published time-weighted returns. Dalbar[2] studies over the last 20 years show *the average investor earns about 40% of the index*. The reality is most people don't have the stomach to be responsible for making global economic decisions when the market sells off 20%-30%. However, if you own well-managed companies you can be confident the management will take advantage and make good decisions.

Hedge funds and private equity

Fortunes have been made by concentrating risk, using leverage, and being right. However, the explosion in the number of alternative investment options has made it much more difficult than in the past. Keep in mind that most hedge funds close inside of five years of launch due to poor performance.

Private equity has the advantage of taking a long-term view, improving management, and providing guidance, as well as capital. This too has become a crowded industry and understanding how returns are calculated takes an advanced math degree. As the wise carpenter says: Measure twice before you cut.

It takes high conviction, steadfastness

In order to capture the higher returns associated with equity investing, investors need to have conviction in their strategy so they can remain invested through the inevitable downturns. If you have what it takes, do it yourself. If you don't, hire a firm or an advisor who meets the criteria and will do it for you.

---

1   DealBook Conference 2015. The Other Investors' Perspective. Druckenmeyer, Stanley. November 3, 2015. https://www.youtube.com/watch?v=l0YjPekmccs.

2   Quantitive Analysis of Investment Behavior. 2015. http://www.dalbar.com/ProductsampServices/AdvisorsSolutions/QAIB/tabid/214/Default.aspx.

CAVEAT EMPTOR

LIMITATIONS OF MORNINGSTAR RANKINGS AND ASSET ALLOCATION OPTIMIZATION

I have seen a lot of good concepts get repurposed, which, in turn, led to disappointing results. This essay is intended to help you avoid making, or being led to make, false assumptions that can lead to bad decisions.

Good information poorly used

When Morningstar introduced mutual fund research and rankings over 30 years ago, it was a wonderful tool. It was an objective presentation of returns, portfolio composition, fees, and other important information. With good intention, they introduced their Star Ranking System. This system ranked funds into categories based generally upon their historical risk-adjusted returns. A five-star ranking was the gold standard and every fund that achieved it spared no expense marketing the good news. Unfortunately, disappointment often followed.

Studies have shown the performance of mutual funds following Morningstar awarding a five-star ranking have been below average and, in many cases, substantially below. This varies from year to year and from study to study, but the warning is clear. Past performance is no indication of future performance.

Things have improved a lot since then but it highlights that good tools can be used incorrectly and lead to poor results. In order to use them effectively, one must know what those limitations are.

Asset Allocation Optimization (AAO)

Modern Portfolio Theory (MPT), which was developed back in the 1950s, was truly innovative and is the basis for most current asset allocation recommendations. It has done wonders to help people understand and limit risk in their investment portfolios. MPT is a thoughtful process to help lessen concentrated risk by diversifying assets. The theory still holds, however; the application of the theory, which requires inputs and estimates, can produce very different outcomes.

Studies[3] from leading institutions point out that diversification usually reduces risk over longer periods of time, but does not guarantee less risk. Importantly, historical relationships between asset classes do not always hold, especially over shorter periods. Asset allocation optimization uses literally hundreds of assumptions. The recommendations produced can be only as good as the inputs. Like statistics or a loaded gun, in the right hands you are safer. In poorly trained hands, you might assume a false sense of confidence and be at greater risk.

Good, but not science

The wealth management industry has taught advisors that, in order to have a well-diversified portfolio, one needs to own a lot of different assets classes: Large stocks, small stocks, international stocks, emerging market stocks, bonds of every quality and maturity, and commodities. The extrapolation of the sound advice is "the more the better." The challenge is when people start grouping investment strategies with very different structures and return patterns into homogenous "asset classes." Hedge funds come to mind. There are dozens of different types and they behave very differently.

Another "asset class" that can be found in many asset allocation models is Real Estate Investment Trusts. This subset of stocks is, generally speaking, small cap value stocks with special tax treatment. Master Limited Partnerships (MLPs) and Treasury Inflation Protected Securities (TIPS) are just two

---

3   Back to the Drawing Board. John Ferry and Mike Foster. The Wall Street Journal. April 12, 2010. www.wsj.com/articles/SB10001424052702303960604575158141978114692.

of many categories in asset allocation models, of which the value of their inclusion is unclear.

Clarity or confusion

I recently saw a proposal from one of the world's largest banks suggesting there were 26 different equity asset classes. Really? It begs the question: If the 26 equity asset classes have materially different investment patterns, or if the institution was trying to create dependency on their financial advisors?

A full explanation is beyond the scope of this essay, but the message is simple: Diversification is good, but excess diversification does not assure increased returns. Past correlation among asset classes does not assure the same future correlation, especially during times of duress and big market corrections.

"Toto, I've a feeling we're not in Kansas anymore."

— Dorothy, *Wizard of Oz*

Interest rates have declined for the last 35 years. In July of 2016, interest rates were so low that one-third of the world's government bonds were at *negative interest rates*. That means you have to pay them to borrow your money. How many of the economic models on which we rely to produce asset allocation forecasts have factored in negative interest rates in their historical projections? Did Markowitz? You can bet the "science" of asset allocation optimization, as promoted by the lesser informed, is based, at least in part, on best guesses about future correlations.

Does this mean the conclusions have no validity? No, but beware of the advisor who doesn't understand the nuances and recommends a bond portfolio instead of cash to "reduce risk." I have heard even tenured advisors stand firm in their position that "over the long term" it will work out. I can assure you that when poor performance persists, these same advisors will be fired before long, and their term will be over.

Unaudited experience invites risk

I am reminded of one of my father-in-law's favorite adages of "rising confidence that stems from unaudited, clinical experience." In English, this means that the practitioner has rising confidence in their opinion because, from their personal experience, things have always turned out a certain way. The longer the trend lasts in the experience of that one person, the more confident they are and the more dangerous their advice becomes. "I have been coming here for thirty years and it has never rained on a Tuesday."

Words to remember: When investing, we are dealing with human behavior, not physical sciences.

Family Foundation or Investment Committee Investing

How to make it work for you

———◆•◆———

I have consulted to and served on dozens of boards and investment committees overseeing billions in assets. Having been on both sides of the table, I have seen the benefits and limitations of investment committees and know what works. With the humility of a politician, below are thoughts on how to expedite the process and get better results.

If it is your foundation

If this is your family foundation, you get to choose how involved your members should be. Two questions to contemplate: 1) do you know enough to be able to assess who you want to oversee the investments, and 2) how involved do you want to be in tactical decisions? Unless you are an investment pro, my advice is to direct the strategic decisions and delegate the tactical implementation to proven professionals.

Joining an investment committee

Congratulations, you are respected for your good judgment and financial acumen. Many of your committee members are financial industry veterans while others have a keen interest. What you want to know at the outset, in addition to making sure there is adequate E&O insurance, is how involved will the committee be in tactical investment decisions? Two points of evaluation:

1. **Is the committee strategic or tactical?** Some committees are heavily involved in the strategic decisions like asset allocation, spending policies, and risk exposures, and then delegate the implementation. Others get deeper into the process and review individual manager selection and conduct quarterly performance analysis. These tactical committees usually retain the ability to replace the managers as well as control of the timing of asset allocation shifts.

2. **Pros and cons to both approaches.** Before you accept, look for a committee who works well together and is not loaded with people who fancy themselves as the next Warren Buffett, John Bogle, or Ray Dalio. History has shown overly involved investment committees tend to slow down the process, micro manage the investment team, and detract from results.

Delegating the day-to-day oversight

Outsourced Chief Investment Officer (OCIO). If you want to manage the big picture and delegate the investment responsibility and accountability, find a firm that will accept full fiduciary responsibility. Effectively, you hire a firm to be your Chief Investment Officer who is empowered to make all investment decisions in keeping with your objectives. This should be a formal process when dealing with large assets. With family assets it can be less formal but should include all of the essential elements. The evaluation of your OCIO is pretty straightforward.

   a. Did they follow your objectives as laid out in your investment policy?

   b. Was the service and communication good?

    c.   Were the risk-adjusted returns good, bad, or acceptable?

Avoid arrangements where the OCIO can have an economic bias when recommending asset allocation or using proprietary investment strategies.

Selecting an investment consultant

If you want more involvement, investment consultants are the way to go. They are involved in every step of the process but stop short of implementation. They make recommendations to the committee, which then decides whether or not to accept the recommendation. Below are steps to follow if your organization is searching for a new consultant.

1.   **Update your Investment Policy Statement.** Spend time on the section that dictates how the investment consultant will be evaluated. Committees that retain the right to adjust asset allocation and money managers need to understand that they will be responsible in large measure for the investment results — good and bad.

2.   **Choose investment consultant type.** Independent consultants are different from brokerage firm consultants, money managers, trust companies, and commercial bank consultants. Each brings benefits and baggage. Large companies can offer breadth, depth, and pricing efficiencies, but bureaucracy may accompany them. Big independent consulting firms may require hundreds of millions in assets to get their attention. Large independent consultants are very different than small independent firms, who often align with custodial partners to provide services. These alignments usually come with soft dollar support, which are normal business practices, but need to be disclosed and understood.

3.   **Avoid simply reusing an old Request for Proposal (RFP) and sending it to a dozen financial organizations that board members know.** Rather, if you spend time drafting a thoughtful RFP that is tailored to your needs, you should get respondents who are well qualified to do what you want.

4. **No more than five.** Once you understand which organizations are most likely to be a good fit, only send requests to that group. It should be fairly easy for an experienced committee to limit the number of recipients to five, as any more than that is not likely to add additional insight or value.

Streamline requests for proposals, please

5. **More is less.** In the absence of knowing what is really important, a growing trend in RFPs is to ask for everything. This practice is so entrenched that most firms have large departments ready to kick out volumes of data in language that satisfies the compliance departments but may offer limited illumination to the requestor.

6. **In addition to the boilerplate.** A few things worth knowing about the proposed investment consulting team:

   a. Do they personally have clients similar to you?

   b. What is the depth of the team's experience?

   c. What is their current contrarian view?

   d. Have they published relevant thought leadership pieces?

   Firms that respond to your questions directly, as opposed to generically, indicate they are paying attention and may offer better service. Firms that simply cut and paste responses and include attachments that are off-point may not be a good fit.

Evaluating a consulting relationship

7. **Pre-plan reviews and criteria.** Surprisingly, few investment committees determine in advance how they will evaluate their satisfaction with their investment consultant. An OCIO is held responsible for investment results, whereas the invest-

ment consultant should be responsible for the process and recommendations that lead to the results.

8. **Set expectations.** If you have a consulting relationship, determine in advance what you expect of the consultant. Investment results should be reviewed each quarter but can only be fairly evaluated after several years. Consider the following criteria to evaluate overall satisfaction in the interim.

Six-month review

a. **Administration:** Did the account set-up and transition go smoothly? Were expectations met regarding reporting, statements, online access, cash transfers?

b. **Investments:** Was the reinvestment of assets orderly and did it go as planned? Were investment restrictions (SRI/ESG) carried out?

c. **Communication:** Was it professional, too much content, or too little? Were all appropriate parties kept informed?

One-year review

a. **Administration:** Is the staff relationship good? You should experience polite, professional, and responsive staff. Are day-to-day issues such as cash flow and disbursements handled well?

b. **Investments:** Are SRI mandates adhered to? If violations, was there a timely resolution? Is the volatility within the expected ranges? Have managers performed in line with expectations? Are performance reviews and reporting materials as promised?

c. **Communication:** Do investment committee members feel involved and understood? Is the consultant proactive? Has the quality of firm communications, including webcasts, market updates, SRI related, etc., met expectations?

Two-year review

a. **Administration:** Has it been excellent?

b. **Investments:** Are managers performing as expected? Have asset allocation recommendations/shifts been well-communicated? Have manager changes been thoughtful and timely? Rebalancing – was it done, has it worked?

c. **Communication:** Does the committee feel the consultant listens to, and responds well to, their issues? Is the right amount of time spent on the most important topics?

Three-year review

After the third year, investment results should reflect the quality of the consultant's investment recommendations. Consider the following:

a. **Clarity of recommendations:** Consider the market, economy, asset allocation, and managers.

b. **Have forecasts been well reasoned:** Have the range of potential outcomes been accurate?

c. **Volatility and performance:** Have they been in line with expectations?

Two pet peeves

1. **The ability to "be nimble."** At the risk of offending users of this tired expression, if an investment consultant claims to be or wants to be "nimble," they are in the wrong business. In-

stitutions think in terms of decades and should position their portfolios for trends, not trades. The requirement to be nimble should be reserved for portfolio managers, OCIOs, and hedge fund traders.

2. **"To hedge fund or not, that is the question."** Stemming from a strategy developed in the late 1940s to limit losses during bear markets, hedge funds have evolved into a trillion-dollar business that some observers claim are now primarily a way to turn liquid assets into Greenwich, CT, real estate. With annual management fees at 2% and a 20% profit participation, excellence still exists; it's just harder to find compelling results, net after fees.

Whether you oversee your family foundation or sit on an investment committee, the process to get the right investment relationship in place is very similar. Knowing what and who to look for will greatly improve your probability for success.

GET GREAT SERVICE FROM YOUR WEALTH ADVISOR

KNOW WHAT TO EXPECT AND HOW TO GET IT

———————•·•———————

Every new client relationship requires a leap of faith on both sides. The client hopes the new advisor gives sound advice, good service, competitive returns, and sees the family through good and bad times. The advisor hopes the family is patient through difficult markets and stays long enough to recoup the sunk costs of onboarding a new relationship.

Few clients know what great service entails and how to be sure to receive it. Establishing proper expectations will help you get experience you deserve and create the long-lasting, gratifying relationship the advisor seeks. If your family's investable assets are over $30MM you should receive all of what follows. If your net worth is less, you should still receive most of the services.

Have regular review cycles

Formal meetings should occur two or three times a year, if possible, with interim updates as needed. Meetings should include a financial review and investment update. Comprehensive investment analysis and relative performance assessment should occur annually. A deep dive more frequently is less informative than one might suspect and can encourage short-term behavior. An in-depth discussion of the following topics should be rotated.

Fiduciary review

1. **Trust officer checklist.** Established families have estate plans in place that should be reviewed and updated periodically. Families of size and complexity should have a checklist of items to review annually that may include "Crummey" letters, disbursements, charitable remainder trust or loan payments, amongst other things. Maintain a list of these items, as well as who is responsible for seeing they get done. If someone else drops the ball, you are still left holding the bag.

2. **Estate planning review.** The composition of the family holdings and structures will drive what should be reviewed and how frequently. Changes in tax law and family dynamics will drive what new items should be considered and when. Keep a list of who is responsible for each aspect. Have a plan to confirm completion of required items.

3. **Compliance: State, local, and federal.** Before meetings, your advisors should check for tax law updates or changes that may affect the family. Most changes are minor and infrequent. Regardless, one of your advisors should be tasked with the responsibility as part of their process.

4. **Continuing education.** Timely and relevant briefs should be included for further reading. Staying current on important topics is part of stewardship and must be practiced in order for succeeding generations to value and follow suit. Your advisory team shouldn't swamp you with an endless stream of white papers. It should be tailored to your interests and aspirations.

Stewardship and family

Your advisory team should help you structure these meetings and can lead discussions.

5. **Mission statements.** Families with a long-term vision often want to capture their values and philosophies in a statement. Crafting a few sentences reflecting, "who we are and what we stand for" is a simple and remarkably fulfilling exercise. As affluence and progeny expand, so will the importance of this statement. Revisiting the language every decade or so makes sense.

6. **Family philanthropy.** Whether a donor advised a fund, a family foundation, or writing checks (God forbid), an annual review of the documentation, filings, tax returns, and administrative issues is important. This review can be done in a couple of hours or over a seminar-driven weekend.

7. **Multi-generational involvement can begin as early as the teen years.** Over time, responsibilities of the family philanthropy and finances should shift to the adult children. Knowing the administrative requirements is the common, if least interesting, first stage of the journey. I remember I had to wash the family car for a few years before I was allowed to drive it.

8. **Grant review process can be formal or informal.** Learning how to handle requests for money from friends and neighbors is a valuable life lesson. Instituting a formal grant request process, or just having a discussion about how to respond, is time well spent.

9. **Impact of past gifts.** If a process exists, measure the impact of past gifts regularly. The exercise introduces a discipline of measuring results that has lasting value across a multitude of areas.

10. **Investment reviews and white papers.** Exposing the family to vocabulary and investment concepts regarding the family foundation is part of stewardship development. Socially Responsible Investing (SRI), Environmental and Governance (ESG), and Impact Investing (II) are important social topics and merit understanding by all. Eventually, the family's affluence will be the children's responsibility. Having ten or fifteen years of practice increases the probability of success.

Tax planning and compliance

11. **Tax law changes, organizational reviews.** Every year, have your advisors review legislative updates and court rulings on companies, partnerships, pass-through entities, and trusts. Awareness of tax implications is part of sound planning and will save money and aggravation. Certain structures are better suited for control, protection, and tax treatment. Things change and people forget. Refresh regularly.

12. **Budgets.** Setting and keeping budgets is a best practice that not every family sticks to. In fact, few even try. However, everyone should review cash flow needs for living expenses, tax payments, capital expenditures, and charitable and investment commitments. If you incorporate this as a part of the regular review process it should help keep checkbooks balanced. What gets measured gets managed.

13. **Corporate actions.** Check that all documents of the various family legal structures and operating agreements are current and minutes of meetings are recorded and filed. It is a good time to ensure items such as signatories, electronic passwords, and beneficiary designations are in good order.

Investment reviews

14. **Investment policy and reporting.** As referenced at the outset, a deep dive on investments should be conducted annually and it starts with the governing document — an investment policy statement (IPS). The IPS should include responsibilities, asset allocation, risk exposure, income needs, fee competitiveness, and absolute and relative performance expectations.

15. **Relative performance, risk containment.** Investment management organizations change regularly and it is as important to understand why a firm performed the way it did, as it is to know how well they performed. To a large extent, asset allocation determines results, so be sure you are where you should be. Review the liquid assets, stocks, bonds, and

cash, in conjunction with real estate and direct private investments. A balanced approach fosters stability and protects during recessions.

16. **Internal rates of return.** Relative performance tells you how the money manager did. Internal return calculations tell you how well you did. The difference is usually attributed to the timing of cash flows. If the variance is large, know why.

17. **Cash flow and year-end tax planning.** As the saying goes: For the wealthy, April 15th is not tax day, every day is tax day. A discussion should include anticipated or unusual tax incidents that merit proactive action. For example, if stock market losses occur or if a new business will show early losses, gains might be harvested from other assets to offset. Similarly, specific assets such as intellectual property, partnerships, farm, or energy holdings can be subject to special tax treatment.

Risk and insurance review

18. **Scope and terms.** Periodically, have your insurance professional review your exposure and coverage. Ask where gaps exist and avoid overlaps. After stock market corrections, verify the continued viability of universal life insurance policies. Checklist:

  • Carrier due diligence

  • Property and casualty, umbrella liability

  • Medical, health, long term care

  • Cyber, information, and online security

  • Personal: Fine art, kidnapping, identity theft, aircraft, offshore, captive insurance vehicles, new concepts

Using one carrier can reduce costs, ease the claims process and help with coverage of disputes.

Document roundup

Maintain a list of important documents, instructions, and their location.

- Wills, trusts, tax forms, partnership, deeds

- Titles, warranties, tax returns

- Healthcare proxies, final instructions, marriage, birth and baptismal certificates, and pre-nuptial agreements

- Military service

FAMILY

"The love of family and the admiration of friends is much more important than wealth and privilege."

— Charles Kuralt

Family Philanthropy Breeds Harmony

A Step-by-Step Guide for You and Your Family

———————◆●◆———————

Working with many hundreds of families to define and achieve their philanthropic aspirations, I have seen what works. Families who use a thoughtful process can groom future leaders, foster stewardship, and give back to the community all at the same time.

The basics of family philanthropy:

1. **Decide what causes you want to support.** Education, medical, and religious are among the most common recipients. Whatever you support, giving advance thought to whom and why you want to give is smart. Doing so goes a long way to help you and your children know how to respond when approached for donations. It is easier to decline a request that is outside of your pre-defined parameters than it is to just say "no." The former method lets people know you are thoughtful about your philanthropy and are not rejecting them personally if you decline their solicitation.

2. **Maximize your charitable dollars.** The tax code allows for contributions of appreciated assets with unrealized, and there-

fore untaxed, gains. In order to maximize your charitable impact, establish a fund that can receive appreciated assets (more later). Avoid writing checks from your personal account.

3. **Consider donor-advised fund of foundations.** There are many types of charitable vehicles, each with unique tax treatment and limitations. These include many estate-planning techniques, which will not be discussed here. I will only list a few of the more common choices that offer greater opportunity for family involvement.

    a. **Donor-advised funds** are probably the most popular. Offered by many mutual fund companies, the donor contributes liquid securities, i.e. stocks, bonds, mutual funds, or cash into a fund. The donor then "recommends" a recognized charity to receive funds. As long as the IRS recognizes the organization as a qualified charity, the recommendation is granted.

    b. **Community foundations.** This is very similar to the donor-advised mutual fund option above, but may allow the donor a little more influence over how the funds are managed and may offer more public recognition supporting the local community.

    c. **Private family foundations.** Allows for more control over many aspects of the management and disbursement of funds, but requires more oversight, and usually a lower tax deduction. Family foundations are more common with larger gifts. They also can offer an element of insulation from unsolicited requests for donations.

Involving the family

The level of formality is less important than communicating and following a few important steps.

Have a charitable mission statement. Writing few sentences on the purpose of the funds is really important. It sets the stage for why money is being donated and to whom. Families who desire participation from multiple age groups are wise to incorporate feedback from all participants. People in their 20s often want to support causes different from those in their 70s. Families with a variety of interests should list several areas to support. This signals everyone's perspective is valued. The more inclusive the process, the more effective it will be in the long run.

Explain the administration. A few sentences on who is responsible for the paperwork are a good idea. This can include family members or external advisors and doesn't need to complicate matters. Rotating the responsibilities every few years broadens the involvement and educates in the process.

Grant-making objectives. Write down how much you plan to annually give away, who will get the money, and who and how it will be decided. It is also worth a sentence or two noting whether or not you plan to try to measure impact of your contributions and, if so, how.

Administration and investments

Family philanthropy is an excellent training ground to prepare the next generation for the less glamorous but essential aspects of affluence.

Finances, forms, and filings. When a charitable fund is established there are forms to file and investment decisions to be made. Use the process as a teaching opportunity. Learning the vocabulary and concepts can take years to master, so start early and go slowly.

Red flags and limitations. The IRS has strict criteria as to what expenses can and cannot be borne by the foundation. If you establish a family foundation, be especially careful. Consult tax advice to avoid unintended misuse of funds. It can be embarrassing if it becomes known outside of the family and may put the viability of the entity at risk of disqualification. Salaries to family members and travel to exotic destinations are always closely scrutinized.

Traditions

Families with charitable inclinations often use the foundation as one more way to bring everyone together. Traditions can be formal or informal and can range from destination family meetings to simply being included in discussions. Asking the next generation about the traditions they would like to start for their future families is always a lively discussion.

Avoid the classic trap

Parents who want children's involvement, but won't cede control can create ill will. The classic example is where Mom and Dad want to support the ballet, museum, or opera, while the children want to support environmental initiatives. One way to deal with differing ideas is to establish segments of the foundation that will be allocated to specific interests.

Success story for handling changes

After selling a successful business, two parents followed their passion and established a foundation dedicated to building small gardens in blighted, urban neighborhoods. They established a grant process where requests would be considered, awarded, and funded for the building of beautiful "open spaces." As their children came of age, the parents wanted the adult children to take over the reins of the family foundation.

After a year of being in charge, the children went to Mom and Dad with an observation and recommendation. Creating these open spaces was a noble cause, but it just was not the passion of the children. The children recommended they spend all the money and get it all in place right away. The public would get much more immediate benefit as opposed to trickling it out over a 20-year period. At first the parents were upset, but it soon turned into pride because of the way their children handled the conversation.

Successful families talk with each other

Family foundations can and should be more than a planning tool to reduce income and estate taxes. Studies have shown that the primary reason families gave in describing their own wealth transitions as successful was good communication among the family, not high investment returns or clever tax strategies.

No family is immune to the risk of discord. When weekly Sunday dinners are no longer an option due to time and distance, family philanthropy can play a pivotal role in fostering harmony today and for years to come.

SUCCESSFUL WEALTH TRANSITIONS: INFORM, INVOLVE, ENTRUST

HOW TO PREPARE CHILDREN FOR STEWARDSHIP WHILE BRINGING THE FAMILY CLOSER TOGETHER

———————●•●———————

Families who use a thoughtful process can prepare the next generation for their roles as stewards and bring the family closer together.

The basics of transition

Parents of all eras have struggled with the decision of when to let "the kids" know about the family finances. There is no simple answer, but at some point the next generation needs to know, and it is better for Mom and Dad to plan when and how to bring the children into the loop, rather than having them learn about family finances from the internet. Or worse, in the midst of a crisis.

Thoughtful communication is at the heart of successful wealth transitions. Helping the next generation become effective stewards is a process and one that requires time and commitment from all parties. Understanding the importance of keeping family matters private, as well as setting expectations about the role of financial assets in their future, are two factors. So how does one begin the journey? One step at a time.

Stages of wealth transition

1. **Inform:** At what age does one begin to share some of the family's financial picture so that the children get a sense of future responsibilities? How does one prepare another for stewardship?

2. **Involve:** When should children be part of the conversation so they can begin to understand the legal, tax, and investment issues, as well as the needs and viewpoints of other family stakeholders?

3. **Entrust:** When should responsibilities and control be transferred? In what proportions? To whom?

A comprehensive and well-executed communication and education process will take time. Some families begin early and spread it out over a decade or more. Others start much later and accelerate the stages. Each family is unique and the right plan will depend on the complexity of the family and the disposition and capabilities of the next generation.

Each family is unique

1. **Families with private operating businesses** face additional issues, such as company management and succession, voting control, budget allocations, bonus implications, equity ownership, distribution preferences and liquidity. There is too much here to cover in this context. Let's just agree it's complicated.

2. **Capable *and* interested.** Families with children who are not interested, not capable, or not yet responsible enough may need to consider fiscal oversight and — importantly — communicate the reasons and rationale in advance. In the latter two situations, it can be a tough conversation.

3. **Avoid sibling no-win situations.** Making one sibling the trustee for another is almost always a bad idea.

4. **Blended families** and challenged spousal relationships have their own set of circumstances that require special planning and communication.

Your first guidepost is to inform

1. **They already know.** Children have a pretty good understanding of the family's affluence at an early age. When parents tell them that they will be included in discussions regarding private family matters, they will probably feel good about the vote of confidence. It takes a long time to learn the vocabulary and even longer to grasp how to apply the concepts. Reinforcing that the education will occur over several years and the purpose is to help prepare them should alleviate anxiety.

2. **Prepare for independent living.** The process should help prepare children for the normal responsibilities: Getting a job, budgeting, saving for retirement, marriage, and children. The process can begin as early as the mid-teens. If delayed, some benefits may be missed. There have been instances when the children thought there was a large family fortune they would inherit. When the disappointing facts were revealed, resentment ensued.

Eye dropper, teaspoon, glass

1. **It is probably best to go slowly.** Families often have children attend a family meeting where some aspects of the finances are revealed. It helps to have advisors review legal, tax, or investment issues. This puts the family members on the same side of the table learning together and avoids the teacher/pupil dynamic. If a parent is doing all of the talking, it can cause tension in some families.

2. **Formal seminars.** Others have children attend sponsored programs with other "next-gen" attendees. Both methods begin the exposure to issues and the awareness of the need for further education.

Your second guidepost is involvement

1. **Time for input.** Once the next-gen is "in the know" and you have confidence about their conduct, it is time to encourage input. It is a good idea to establish at the outset how their input will be received and acted upon. Parents who miss this step risk having young adults expecting to have an equal say in the family's finances far before Mom and Dad are ready.

2. **Family philanthropy as a proving ground.** Often families use philanthropy as the "test" vehicle. Empowering the next-gen to engage in the disposition of funds, as well as participating in the investment decisions, enables the parents to see the progression of each child. Letting the younger generation know that mistakes are inevitable and learning from those mistakes is one of the goals. This is covered extensively in a prior chapter.

Your third guidepost is to entrust

1. **Your goal for your children is for them to become responsible, ethical, educated, and independent.** Once a member of the next generation has exhibited these traits, and if the family's financial situation allows, management of funds, if not outright ownership, should be considered.

2. **Your goal should be to be the chairperson, not the CEO.** The grooming process of preparing children to assume responsibility takes time but it fosters understanding among siblings (and spouses), minimizes surprises, and is worth the effort. Allowing adult children to assume control of some of the family's finances, knowing they are armed with a decade or two of

experience, and not having to worry about every decision is a wonderful position to be in.

Start planning now

However you decide to inform and involve your heirs, it will go more smoothly if you have a plan. When done well, you will strengthen and improve relationships among the family along the way.

It Takes More Than Trust to be a Good Trustee

MASTERING THE TRICKS OF CHOOSING A TRUSTEE

What a trust is

A trust is a legal entity created by the "grantor," a/k/a the person who contributes the assets and decides on the terms, for a specific purpose.

What a trustee does

A trustee is the legal representative who controls the trust and is empowered to carry out the terms for the benefit of the beneficiaries. There are many types of trusts and hundreds of ways they can be structured. For illustration purposes, let's assume that assets are put in trust for the general benefit of children or grandchildren.

Trustee selection does not have to be tricky

What should you consider? There are three primary options — family, friend, or financial institution. Who should be the family's trustee is among the most important decisions a family must make. The inclination to select a family member or family friend is high, but corporate trustees are also a viable choice to consider.

- **Family or friend.** When a non-professional is named trustee, the assumption going in is that they understand the family dynamics and will "do the right thing" if extenuating circumstances arise. They may also choose to not charge a fee to the trust so it may be less expensive. However, requirements of the trustee are extensive, and unless the trustee has reasonable knowledge of the requirements, or commits to learning it, the pitfalls could outweigh the benefits. Secondly, the ability or capacity of the named individuals may diminish or the relationship with the family may go sour years after they were named. It happens, believe me.

- **Corporate trustee.** Trust departments are knowledgeable about the laws, restrictions, and requirements. If they do something wrong, there is a deep pocket to make it right and they will be around in thirty or forty years when the terms of the trust need to be followed. That is why they charge fees. However, unless your relationship is large, the service can be impersonal and the individual administrator often rotates regularly.

Let's go back—a little history first

As recently as forty to fifty years ago, it was common for people to open a trust relationship with a local bank and when the parents died the institution managed the money and charged fees for decades. *It was a **very** good business.* Additionally, the language of the documents the trust companies provided made it difficult or near impossible for the trust department to be removed. That created an uninterruptable ongoing revenue stream. Good for them, but how about the client?

People got lazy. When you know the clients can't leave regardless of investment returns or service levels, things can go poorly for the client. And they did. Eventually, courts required the trust departments to relinquish control and those practices are long gone.

Today, things are a lot better. Almost all new trust documents allow the trust to be moved from one institution to another quite easily. Most documents specify how a trustee can be changed and trust companies have realized the short-term revenue gains achieved by keeping business against the desires of the beneficiaries are not worth the reputational damage.

Factors to guide selection

- **Complexity, size, and horizon.** Common factors guiding the trustee selection are the trust's complexity, size, and the expected time horizon. If the trust or trusts own significant assets to benefit many generations, it likely will require subjective assessments in the future. For this reason, a professional trustee can be very helpful. Stories of well-intended family friends serving as trustee, and being too hard, too soft, or negligent fill volumes (and court dockets). On the other hand, the poor reputation earned by large bank trust departments over the years are equally numerous. So what is one to do?

- **If the non-professional is chosen,** the first course of action is to have a qualified lawyer explain the terms, requirements, and expectations to all concerned. The second is to have a mechanism in place to regularly ensure all that should be done is being done: Required distributions, waiver letters, tax return filings, and proper documentation of requests, deliberations, and decisions.

- **Schedule annual or bi-annual meetings** with the drafting trust attorney, trustee(s), and beneficiaries present. At this meeting, the trust attorney should review the terms of the trust, conditions for disbursements, and offer general updates to all concerned. This allows the beneficiaries direct access to an informed neutral party and should reinforce the actions and decisions of the trustee, if any are in doubt.

- **Corporate trustee.** If a professional trustee or corporate trust company is selected, a few considerations to heed include:

- **Co-trustees.** Name a family friend and a corporate trustee to work together. It doesn't save any money, but it helps ensure taxes will be filed on time and any non-standard disbursements will be handled correctly. It also affords the individual trustee "air cover" if discretion is required and requests are denied. *This is my clear favorite option.*

- **Replacing your trustee.** Ensure there are provisions and a process in the trust document to replace the corporate trustee with a qualified successor trustee. This encourages good service. Today, the better trust companies will not accept an assignment without this type of provision. If an unpopular decision is rendered by the corporate trustee, odds are pretty good it is driven by law and not motivated by retaining assets on which to bill fees.

- **Trust protectors.** Consider appointing a "trust protector." This is most often an individual who is empowered to be informed of the activities of the trust and can advise beneficiaries. This can carry an additional expense and complexity, but in larger situations is a good option to have.

How to avoid being "hit up" from family

This tactic is especially valuable when one family member is substantially wealthier than others and is regularly being asked to pay for the misfortunes of relatives. Consider establishing a "buffer trust." This is where you put money in a trust to take care of unspecified future family needs. Tell your relatives the trust company decides if their request qualifies for support and for how much. This demonstrates your concern for family members, yet gets you off the hook for individual decisions. There are a few twists involved, so ask your tax and estate attorney how to do it.

Final thought

The financial and emotional costs of an incorrectly administered trust can be very high. Tax penalties, disqualification, or litigation can be expensive and emotionally draining. More importantly, misunderstandings among family members, especially a generation down the line, can be devastating. As the size, complexity, and time horizon of the trust increases, the importance of proper communication and administration becomes exponential. The selection of the right trustee — either personal or professional — is as important as the terms of the trust. Make the decision wisely.

EXECUTOR'S GUIDELINES

HOW TO DIVIDE WITHOUT CONQUERING*

———————•●•———————

There are a lot of important but relatively easy things that should be done before an executor is called into service. The suggestions that follow are geared toward the executor (or personal representative in some states) being a close family member or the child of a parent. Most of the suggestions should be helpful in all cases. Each state has specific requirements so be sure to know what is required in yours. A few hours of planning and a call or two to an estate attorney can save endless hassles and possibly prevent a lifetime of familial discord.

When you accept the request

1. **Do what you can, while you can.** When you accept the role as executor or co-executor (also referred to as personal representative in some states), there are a handful of things that should be done right away. This can save both time and trouble.

2. **Read the will.** Knowing where the will is and what it contains are essential. You don't need to know all of the details, but you should know what you will be expected to do. Ask if there are any unusual or specific provisions. If the instructions aren't clear to you, they won't be clear to others. This is also a good time to find out if any of the potential heirs may

be surprised by the will. This is not the time to solve family problems, but the executor should understand the complexities that might arise.

3. **Know the basics.** Know the names and contact information of the estate attorney, the CPA, the investment advisor or financial company, and the life insurance agent. Find out if burial or cremation is preferred. Should special arrangements be made? Tough conversations are necessary at this time and some day the peace of mind from having them will be recognized.

4. **Safety deposit box.** Become the co-owner of the safety deposit box, if there is one, so you can get into the box on your own signature. Do not rely on a power of attorney. It expires upon the principal's passing.

5. **Living will, healthcare proxy, and powers of attorney.** A living will details a person's preferences regarding medical care if one becomes incapacitated. A healthcare proxy, also known as advance directive, authorizes someone to receive information, advocate for the patient, and make medical decisions if the patient is incapacitated. It should address end of life issues, as well. General powers of attorney, or at least financial powers of attorney, can be of enormous help in times of extended diminishing capacity.

You may not be the person asked to make these decisions, but even so, have the discussion and know where the documents are located.

6. **Professional assistance.** At some point you will want to seek an attorney's assistance. Too many costly mistakes are made by trying to save money.

    You may suggest that a professional executor be named instead if the estate is large or if there are strained relationships among heirs. It may be better for someone else to be the "bad guy" if there is a difficult message to be delivered. Investing in familial harmony is money well spent. In lieu of hiring a professional to be the executor, consider hiring him or her as agent. This is often less expensive and fees can be better negotiated before the death. Statutory fees for executors can be higher.

7. **Special bequests.** Estates of all sizes can have family heirlooms. It is essential for the owner to have advanced discussions with all relevant people to inform them of his/her intentions. These plans should be written because people remember things differently. Clarifying the plans while one is alive is better than burying a time bomb that could create lasting problems.

8. *Create one joint account.* After a person passes, bills will need to be paid and having access to cash for this purpose will make your job much easier. Have enough in the account to take care of a few months' worth of incidentals.

Financial assets considerations

9. **Register individually owned stocks, savings bonds.** It is less common today than it used to be, however, some people still have investments in the form of paper certificates. Check tax returns and bank accounts for direct deposits to see if dividends have been paid and move them into a brokerage account. Replacing lost certificates is never simple and it's even more difficult after the owner has died. You will want to be able to transfer all investment related assets with a single paperwork transaction.

10. **Create a list of assets (a personal financial statement).** Your job will be much easier if there is a list of all assets and liabilities. Ask that one be compiled and include account numbers, ownership titles, property, cars, land, employer retirement, and beneficiary designations, etc. This takes time but the owner knows what to look for and where to find it. Your financial advisor can help with this.

11. **Usernames and passwords.** One significant challenge is to maintain a current inventory of usernames and passwords. Computers, phones, emails, bank accounts, and credit cards all require passwords and this needs to be updated frequently.

Consider asking that username and passwords be categorized into two or three "buckets."

Passwords for non-sensitive things like Facebook can all be the same. Semi-sensitive access such as email and very sensitive information such as financial accounts should be different and updated more frequently. Ask that this information be kept with the estate attorney, locked in a secure place or with a digital security company. In the week following the death, begin reviewing everything.

12. **Seek ongoing advice and updates.** The role of the executor is not to tell the person what to do. However, encouraging the will maker to review things every three or four years is good governance.

Addressing the complex and changing tax laws is beyond the scope of this essay. Although, it is critical to highlight the benefits that optimal tax planning has for families and charities, as recipients of the assets from the deceased.

When there is a death

13. **Day One.** The day the person dies, there are three things to do:

- **Call the funeral home** and make an appointment. They will make arrangements to pick up the deceased.

- **Notify the investment advisor** and ask him or her to collect and print all of the date of death valuations. Also ask to cease any systematic withdrawals going to banks or other places.

- **Get the keys** to the home, consider changing the locks, and don't let anyone in when you are not there. If there are multiple heirs, they are expecting you to make sure everything is present and accounted for. The last thing you want is one of the heirs to start distributing the will proceeds early.

14. Day Two.

- **Notify nursing homes or landlords** and stop subscriptions that will no longer be used. Smaller items like cable and newspapers are not time critical but if you are being charged for a nursing home unit move out ASAP. Long term healthcare insurance will no longer cover it.

- **Ask the funeral home** to contact Social Security to stop future checks. Wait a week and call to confirm. Automatic deposits after death will have to be returned. Request 20 death certificates from the funeral home. This may sound like a lot, but you will need them to transfer financial accounts and real estate holdings, as well as a surprising number of things. Finally, find and re-read the will and instructions.

15. Optional — get a scanner. Most entities will require originals but in situations that do not, they should accept emailed scanned documents. Having an electronic copy of all of your documents, when it was sent, to whom, and knowing it was received can be a big time-saver.

16. Now, go take care of the family. At this point, if you have addressed all of the above, you are off to a great start. Go and spend time attending to the emotional needs of the family.

After the funeral

17. Redirecting mail/change of address. Redirect the mail of the deceased to your address or a PO box to avoid the need for visiting their house/properties on a daily basis to collect bills and other relevant mail. This will be helpful in processing claims against the estate. This is easily done at the post office or online. When you do it online (recommended) you have to "prove" you are the person who died. Most use the decedent's still-active credit card to do so. The Post Office will charge $1.00. Check the box that forwards the mail of "the entire family" to ensure mail addressed to you, the executor, is also forwarded.

18. **After death certificates are received notify all companies sending pension checks — both physical and automatic deposits — and ask them to stop.** They will request a copy of the death certificate; don't hesitate to see if they will take a copy (as it will be an odd size or two pages due to it not being on a standard size), as those originals become more valuable than what you might suspect. Also remember: Every payment after death will have to be repaid and that can be a real hassle, certainly an extra burden that you want to avoid, if possible.

19. **Bank accounts.** Find the checks and statements and notify the bank that the decedent has passed away. If you are not co-owner, the bank will freeze the account(s) immediately. Fortunately, all checks written prior to the e of death will be honored. You will need to set up an "Estate of" bank account.

20. **Accessing the safe deposit box.** If you are not the co-owner, you will need to ask the bank for the procedures in your state. Generally, you will need certain documentation such as a death certificate, the will, a marriage certificate, executor appointment, AND that you are the spouse, executor, or descendent, for access to be granted. The requirements vary by state, so call the bank before you go to verify what is needed.

21. **Which bank should be used to handle finances?** Decide if you want to use the decedent's bank or your own. If you want to change banks, it will require two sets of documents, two trips, and an asset transfer. You will need notary services and medallion guarantee stamps (more on this later). For ease, many people just choose to use the existing bank.

22. **Register of Wills – what to bring.** Each state has specific steps but the first step everywhere is to have *the will*, not a copy. Then go online to the state website of the decedent's legal residence and read the specific steps and requirements. Typically, you will need:

    • Decedent's Last Will and Testament

    • Decedent's full name, address, and Social Security number

- Death certificate

- Funeral contract or bill

- Estimated value of the estate

- Title to automobiles

- Full names and addresses of all direct decedents and persons named in the will

- Names and address of all the will's witnesses

- Appointment of Resident Agent, if required

- Notice-waiver forms, if applicable

- Your photo ID

23. **Register of Wills.** For starters — and this is important — call ahead! You may need an appointment and, if you live out of state, you may need an in-state (friend or relative) Resident Agent. The Resident Agent form must be *signed before* you go. There are three types of estates: Small, large, and modified — modified means you don't need to file an inventory with the court, which is good. Full accounting can be costly and time-consuming. If there is real estate in another state, find out if there are any special requirements. Finally, decide which bank you will use for the estate checking account ahead of time.

24. **At the Register of Wills.** You want the name of the estate to be the decedent's full name, e.g. "Michael Smith Doe" and use it every time. Also, use your own full name every time. This will avoid confusion or questions regarding initials or middle names.

25. **Letters of Administration.** Get as many as they will give you (ask for at least 12) and wait for them, even if it takes time to avoid having to return. Find out how to get more if needed. If

given blank forms to fill out at home, get two blank copies in case you make a mistake.

26. **Deadlines, notices, and bonding.** Understand the deadlines and the "wait until" dates for forms and filings. Choose a newspaper for the death notice; they will bill you later. This also serves the purpose if people have claims against the estate. There is usually a nominal bond required. Get copies of everything and the contact info of the people with whom you dealt.

27. **After the Register of Wills, before the bank.** You now need to open an "estate of" bank account. However, before this step, you need an Entity Identification Number (EIN). This takes five minutes online and can be done on your phone (even better with a hotspot connection and a laptop). Go to www.irs.gov. Choose the option to download the file as a PDF and bookmark the page. If you plan to open the account that day, email it to your contact at the bank and call to let them know you are coming over.

28. **Old bank.** If you choose to use another bank, notify the old bank right away. Drop off the death certificate and Letters of Administration or let them know they will be mailed. Use UPS, FedEx, or registered mail so they can be tracked and arrive quickly. It is important to ask for all of the accounts in the decedent's name. There may be several, such as a savings account, certificates of deposit, or even accounts in joint name. Get balances and account numbers. With everything paperless these days, be sure to ask.

29. **Open checking account for the estate.** Go to the bank to set up an estate account and move money to pay bills. You will need your Letters of Administration, EIN, and death certificate. If using the same bank, you will probably be able to write a check from the old account to the new. If changing banks, you may need to write a check from your own account to be refunded later. Ask for an ATM card on the account for after-hour deposits and familiarize yourself with the online access.

30. **Real estate in another state.** If real property is owned through a LLC or revocable trust, you may be able to avoid this step. However, if the property is owned in the name of the decedent, an ancillary estate will need to be opened. Find a local lawyer because you will need appraisals and a slew of work to be done.

31. **Find everything.** Go through the past few years' tax returns and look for dividends, interest, K-1s, partnership payments, and automated deposits. Review email accounts.

32. **One-month checklist.** Notify pensions and retirement plans, cancel subscriptions, credit cards, driver's license, utilities, auto and health insurance. Claim life insurance and change beneficiary designations, process surviving spouse Social Security benefits. Review credit cards and cancel continuing subscriptions. Cancel other insurance as appropriate. Add deceased's name to the "Deceased Do Not Contact" list, maintained by the Direct Marketing Association. Notify club and alumni associations and send thank you cards.

33. **Larger estates.** If a valuation of an asset is required (e.g. private company or partnership interest), have the attorney hire the valuation expert to maintain client attorney privilege.

34. **Executor compensation.** Being the executor of an estate takes time and the person can charge a fee. In many family situations, no fee is charged and only expenses such as travel are deducted. However, each state has guidelines as to fair fees. It may make sense to gain concurrence from the family members prior to assessing fees in order to avoid problems. If paying a family member an executor fee becomes an issue, consider hiring professionals instead.

35. **Five mistakes to avoid.**

    a. Don't pick and choose from the instructions in the will.

    b. Don't keep secrets from the family and heirs.

    c. Don't borrow from the estate.

    d. Don't be afraid to ask for or pay for help when you need it.

    e. Pay all debts before distributing proceeds. There can be personal liability if assets are incorrectly distributed, so take your time and do it right.

36. Random tip. Be thoughtful about how to adjust heirs' share of the estate after the heirlooms are distributed. Perceptions of economic value will vary.

What comes next?

At some point, tax returns will need to be filed for the decedent and the estate of the decedent. Seek good tax advice and do what you can as early as you can. The steps that follow the funeral can be tricky, but if done correctly the first time, they need not be overwhelming or frustrating.

* *A special thanks to Mindy Feldman for the loan of her clever title, "How to Divide Without Conquering."*

MANAGING UP AND DOWN

"I have found the best way to give advice to your children is to find out what they want and then advise them to do it."

— Harry S. Truman

Is My Daughter Really Going to Marry That Mimbo?[4]

HOW AND WHEN TO HAVE THE PRE-NUPTIAL CONVERSATION

———————◆•◆———————

In 32 years of experience working with many hundreds of families, the one thing you definitely should know about pre-nuptial conversations is clear: Have it BEFORE your child brings home Betty or Biff.

Pre-nuptials and a spoonful of sugar

Many of my friends have children in their 20s and one asked me recently about the do's and don'ts of pre-nuptial agreements. Not legal advice; rather, how to avoid hurt feelings between the parent and child, as well as avoiding bruising the relationships with the fiancé or the future in-laws.

This is the human part of estate planning. Families of size and complexity have dealt with asset protection and wealth transfer since the beginning of

——————————————

4   Mimbo is a slang term for a male bimbo.

time, but the central issue remains, how do families communicate plans to protect the family's assets?

Bring up the subject

Before your children get in a serious relationship, if possible, talk about it. Your children already know your family is wealthy. They know where you live, vacations you take, boards on which you serve, and the charitable causes you support. They have Googled the assessed value of your home(s) and, if you are a senior executive or director of a public company, they have seen your compensation data and share ownership in government filings.

Tell them you want to have a talk and let them know it is a family discussion on an important topic. Convey that you also want to hear their thoughts. Stay at a high level to educate them. The conversation lets them know you trust them and it prepares them for future conversations with more detail. The age and maturity of the child will drive when and how much information you want to share, but anytime from about sixteen years and up is probably old enough for the initial discussion.

What to say

Your family has been fortunate to accumulate assets and there are plans in place to protect them. The plans are intended to protect the family from any number of things, including spurious lawsuits and unexpected events. You do not need to go into depth, just establish that plans exist and, in most cases, have existed for years. An important concept to reinforce is that these are family assets—not assets they earned.

Let them know that regarding the assets they earn in the future; it will be up to them to decide how they want to handle those. Should they decide to marry, they and their spouse will live independent lives, will support themselves, and assets they accumulate together will be theirs to oversee.

If greater detail is needed

Tell them the family assets are structured to stay in the family and are protected from a variety of unforeseen events such as spurious lawsuits, health problems (alcohol, drugs, and depression), or other adverse events (auto accident, business failures, gambling debts, etc.).

You may choose to say that at some time in the future, they may begin to enjoy some modest income benefit from trusts. It is worth mentioning that their eventual spouse may also come from a family of means and have similar planning in place. If the other family does, your children shouldn't feel targeted or demeaned when they find out.

How will it be received?

Explain to your children that some future spouses will be confident in their financial future and will not be sensitive to signing a pre-nuptial agreement. Others may be more sensitive and feel targeted. Preparing your children early is critical so they know that you are not singling out their current boyfriend or girlfriend for exclusion.

Let your children know that as they get serious in their relationship and are about to become engaged either you or they should raise the topic. It is critical that the future spouse is told that there will be a pre-nuptial agreement before the public announcement of their engagement. It is far easier to deal with any unpleasantness prior to the excitement of planning a wedding.

Talking points for your child to their "about to be betrothed":

    a.   These plans have been in existence for a long time, well before we met.

    b.   The plans protect my family's assets and do not affect our lives or the assets we accumulate together.

    c.   I don't have control over the assets, and even if we object, it won't change things.

    d.   The assets may provide modest income but ultimately will be passed down to grandchildren.

    e.   Our assets and our life are our own, we control our destiny and are not controlled by the terms of any trust or a trustee.

Be prepared to have a conversation with your child and their fiancé to explain what is in place. You do not need to get into specifics, but you should reassure both why the plans are in place. Offer to speak to their parents. Same message, same purpose.

Critical to get it right

Eventually your child's fiancé will need to retain their own lawyer to work through the documents, so if it comes up, be reassuring that this is the normal course of things. Sadly, claims of duress and coercion in signing pre-nups are legendary and have led to agreements being entirely disqualified. The good news is that there are assets and plans that require consideration.

Don't delay

It is ideal if both sides agree that the pre-nuptial agreements will be signed well before the wedding date. Set a date and do not let the date slip. If the lawyers are allowed to wrestle over wording until after the wedding announcements have been mailed, it puts pressure on everyone, and no one wants or needs that. The last thing you want going into the final month of planning your child's wedding is to continue to negotiate a contract that could upset the timing of the marriage.

Who should draft the agreement

A lawyer of course, but who and what type of lawyer? First, it cannot be the same attorney for both parties, as we stressed earlier. Some suggest a family, matrimonial, or divorce lawyer to "best protect" your interests. However, aggressive posturing by the attorney to get the "best protection" can be upsetting and could be ultimately counterproductive. Many suggest using trust and estate lawyers because they know the ins and outs and are accustomed to collaborating to arrive at agreements. It is an important consideration, so choose wisely.

When and where to have the conversation

Encourage your child to set aside time at a public place where the two of them can speak privately. You don't want someone's home to be the scene and permanent reminder of a difficult conversation. Allow for plenty of time to have the conversation in case someone runs late. Plan a specific activity to follow the conversation that is fun and both are looking forward to it. After the conversation, consider going to nice dinner at a favorite restaurant as a way to cap the evening on a high note.

Finally, after dinner don't forget desert! Remember, a spoonful of sugar helps the medicine go down.

DRIVING MR. DAISY

WHEN IS IT TIME FOR DAD TO HAND OVER THE KEYS

———— ●•● ————

In my time as an advisor, I've regularly encountered people coming into unfamiliar responsibilities. Being prepared for events that only happen a once in our life can make things go a whole lot easier on all involved.

True story: "License and Registration"

It was not a question. It was the second time in a week my grandmother was asked. Even worse, it was the same police officer outside her window, staring down at her making the demand.

This is what many of us are destined for. My 83-year-old grandmother, ever so gingerly, backed into another car in the grocery store parking lot. It must have been the favorite grocery store of a lot of senior citizens, because lately there seemed to be a cruiser waiting nearby to referee these all-too-common incidents.

Sensing this might become a pattern, and seeing my four-foot-eleven grandmother's difficulty at seeing over the steering wheel, the officer issued her a summons to appear before a judge to determine if she could keep her driver's license. Fortunately for the shareholders of insurance companies worldwide, and to the dismay of the local auto body industry, the judge said, "no can do."

Although my dad didn't have the conversation leading to the loss of my grandmother's driver's license, he did have to deal with the fallout. For most suburban dwellers, our car is our lifeline. Losing the ability to drive can feel like an amputation. Though we now have Uber and Lyft in many cities to ease getting around, the emotional transition can be enormously challenging.

Introducing the topic

For your mom or dad, the answer of when to give up the keys might be never. However, as vision and motor skills diminish, there may be a time when the topic of planning ahead between an aging parent and their middle-aged child provides an opening. The next time you have a conversation about estate planning, charitable giving, or even quarterly tax planning, consider introducing the topic for a future conversation. Empowering your parent to decide what conditions would merit their decision to stop driving could pave the way for a conversation that doesn't blow up.

Gradual transitions help

Many people have difficulty with driving at night. If this is the case, the next time there is an evening family get-together at one of the children's homes, consider sending a taxi or an Uber to pick Mom or Dad up. Call it a limousine befitting their stature in life. Make it fun. After dinner, drive your parent home personally. This reinforces your relationship and desire to spend time together. Making familiar the eventual solution of using a driving service should help everyone involved.

If there is a concern about personal safety, pay extra to hire a known registered, regular Uber driver, and ask for them by name for future trips. Small gestures are the first step to great progress.

Before THE conversation

If you can, ask the question well in advance. "Mom, how does one know when it is time to stop driving?" Wait for the response. Expect resistance and don't push. "Is it declining vision, the ability to turn and see behind, a loss of hearing?" Timing the conversation around the mention of an ailing friend or an accident on the news may make it less personally directed and more comfortable.

Anchor the issue in their beliefs

No one wants to be controlled or told what to do. We are all more receptive to suggestions that reinforce our beliefs. Work toward establishing agreement on reasons why it would make sense to give up driving. Personal safety may not be enough, but the safety of grandchildren, anyone's grandchildren, may be. Parking lot dents can be ignored, but hitting a mother with a stroller could just be the visual to drive home the point. Have patience; this will take time.

Offer options

Be slow to present a pre-packaged solution to a potential problem that is not acknowledged. Inquire whether Mom or Dad enjoys or tolerates using taxis or driver services. Consider planning outings that involve friends. Have the driver pick up the entire group for dinner. If using a driver service is fun and doesn't carry a stigma or loss of status, acceptance may be easier. Changing patterns can be very difficult, but incorporating friends as part of the new paradigm may ease the transition. Be patient, it may take a few conversations.

Budget

If you can hire a full time driver — wonderful. If not, the expense may not be as high as it once was. Assume there is a need to go somewhere once or twice a day. A driver service may cost an extra $30-40 a day. If you do the math, the cost could add up to another $10-15,000 a year. If that is a lot for your parent, think about putting it on your own credit card or splitting it among your siblings. When you factor in the savings of gas, maintenance, and insurance, the net increase may be less than you expected. Most importantly, the health and safety of all concerned is the reason to do it.

On the day you talk

It may be wise to involve several family members to be part of the conversation. Diffusing resentment is a good reason, but showing support is the better reason. Also having a larger group being part of the solution and new social order helps.
Should you involve an outsider? If you are fortunate enough to have a family friend who your parents respect and trust, they may be helpful.

To have the best possible chance of a smooth transition, the timing and reason for the conversation should be known, if not obvious. A car accident, a health problem, or something Mom or Dad said are good transition points.

No surprises, please

If this is the first time the subject has been raised, it may be a very tough conversation. If it is one of a series of compassionate discussions, and the alternatives to keep Mom and Dad active and involved are known and familiar, you will have a much better chance at reducing dented fenders and keeping the peace at home.

There are no magic bullets, but thoughtful advanced planning, combined with love, compassion, and acceptable alternatives, will go a long way toward keeping family harmony.

READING LIST

The Intelligent Investor
Benjamin Graham, Warren E. Buffett (Preface, Introduction)
Harper & Row; 1985 4th Revised edition

The Little Book That Beats the Market
Joel Greenblatt
John Wiley & Sons, 2010

Capital: The Story of Long-Term Investment Excellence
Charles D. Ellis
Wiley, 2005

What It Takes
Charles D Ellis
Wiley, 2013

Wealth Management Unwrapped
Charlotte Beyer
RosettaBooks, LLC 2014

Preparing Heirs
Roy Williams & Vic Preisser
Robert Reed Publishers, 2010

Where Are All The Customers Yachts?
Fred Schwed, Jr.
Wiley, 2006

The Winner's Circle IV
R.J. Shook
Horizon Publishers, 2005

They Call Me Coach
John Wooden
McGraw-Hill Education, 2003

The Richest Man in Babylon
George S Clason
Signet, 2002

ABOUT THE AUTHOR

Christopher F. Poch is one of Wall Street's leading authorities on managing wealth for ultra high net worth families. He has run international private banking units, advised billionaires and heads of state, has been the chief executive of a trust company, founded the industry-leading UHNW platform, created the industry's most challenging advisor accreditation test, has hosted numerous radio and television shows, and has been quoted widely in the *Wall Street Journal* and *Worth Magazine*.

Of all his career accomplishments the most rewarding has been the positive impact on the families with whom he has worked.

Career affiliations:

- Founder and Global Head, Private Wealth Management, Smith Barney

- Chief Executive Officer, Vice-Chairman of the Board, The Private Trust Company

- Managing Director, Bessemer Trust

Awards and recognitions:

- Thomas Gorman Award for Lifetime achievement, APIC

- Sovereign Military Hospitaller Order of Malta, Board of Councillors

- Co-Founder of Villanova University Delta Student Managed Fund

Mr. Poch lives in Bethesda, MD, with his wife and three daughters.

41783222R00069

Made in the USA
San Bernardino, CA
20 November 2016